I0004663

HOW TO TAG IMAGES

The inquisitory approach to tag selection

Text and images by Greta Faccio

St. Gallen 2019

INTRODUCTION

What are tags?

Tags are keywords used to identify specific features of, in this case, images. By pointing out traits of the image, a list of tags can help to identify the image among many while helping to retrieve it in a long list or a complex database as the internet.

Are tags important?

Tags are extremely important as they convert the image into text and let search engines retrieve them more easily. Tags are crucial to make an image popular! Moreover, users looking for images and visual content might come to it, and thus to your website, through keywords that act as tags for your images. You will find easily a ranking of the most popular tags but remember that these are usually general such as 'dog', 'white', and so on, that they change with the time and the current trends, whereas having specific tags for your image might confer specificity and everlasting interest.

How are tags generated?

Associating a tag or more to images is often led by instinct and creativity, often resulting in a person-to-person difference in tags selection.

WHAT DO YOU SEE?

Physical subjects

Carton

Carton boxes

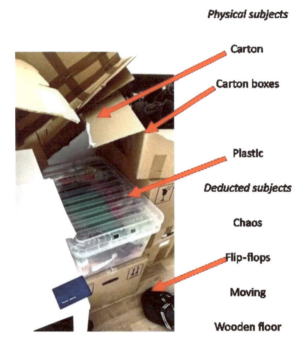

Plastic

Deducted subjects

Chaos

Flip-flops

Moving

Wooden floor

THE INQUISITORY APPROACH

Identifying the main features of an image can be immediate, such as the main subject, the place where the image was taken, a specific monument portrayed. However, many aspects become evident only to a trained eye, after a careful consideration, or after acquiring extensive experience.

The *inquisitory approach* wants to a provide a methodology that can be adopted to identify tags for any picture by analyzing its features in terms of subject, technical characteristics, and in relation to the society. A three-dimensional space is thus created (**Figure 1**) in which images are distributed according to the number of tags used to define them.

In this short pamphlet, tags are classified in three categories, a three-dimensional space for image analysis is presented, and three examples of images are analyzed according to the questionnaire here presented and at the basis of the inquisitory approach.

WHAT DO YOU SEE?

Primary subjects

TV Television Screen

Plant Leaves Pipes Furniture Cable

Secondary subjects

THE INQUISITORY APPROACH –HOW TO

The *inquisitory approach* addresses images according to the three dimensions previously identified (**Figure 1**) by formulating questions that expand the point of view of the compiler.

In the next pages you will see how an image can be subject to multiple questions that leads to the appropriate tags, by referring to both concrete and abstract concepts.

Three examples are presented with the list of questions that help you to identify the single words that best describe the image and that are at the core of the inquisitory approach.

The questionnaire here provided is a standard version that can be expanded to address specific characteristics of the image. The questionnaire is intended to be dynamic and to respond to specific topics, societal changes, interests, and trends.

Examples of questions focusing on the subject are number 1, 4, and 7; on the technical aspects are number 12, 13, and 14; and on the societal aspects are number 20 and 24.

THE THREE-DIMENSIONAL SPACE OF TAGS
A tool to organize images

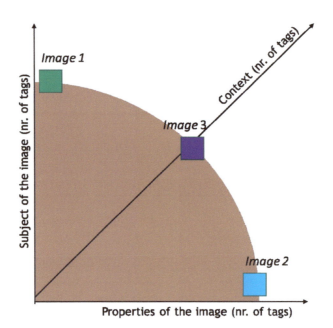

Figure 1 - Tags can be ascribed to three categories:

1. The subject of the image, thus focusing on the features of the primary and secondary objects portrayed

2. The properties of the image, in terms of technical features

3. The context in which the image has been produced and its societal value.

Ideally, an image will be described by an equal number of tags in all three dimensions.

EXAMPLE 1

1. What is the primary subject of the image?
   Flower ramson

2. Are there synonyms to describe the subject? Garlic, buckrams

3. How is the subject called in other languages? Allium ursinum, Aglio orsino, Bärlauch

4. What are the secondary subjects of the image? Wall, leave, stone

5. What is the name of the subjects in other languages? Muro, Stein, Blatt, foglia

6. What is the main color of the subjects? White, green, grey

7. Do the subjects have a specific shape? Star, round, symmetrical

8. In which situation was the image taken? Day, spring

9. Was the image taken in a specific history moment? No

10. Has the subject a specific use nowadays? Gardening, cooking, seasoning

11. Has the subject a traditional use? Cooking, seasoning

12. What's the size of the image? Square

13. What type of image is it? Colour, digital

14. Which capturing device was used? Smartphone, Nokia

15. Is the image edited? Enhanced

16. Are there safety concerns associated? Infection

17. Female/ male subject?   -

18. Where is the subject usually found? Nature, buildings

19. Can you imagine future applications for the subject? Perfume, medicine, painting, aromatherapy

20. Has the image any relation to current events? Urbanization

21. Has the image any relation to past events?
    Overbuilding

22. Do you associate specific smells with the
    subject? Garlic

23. Which feelings does the image inspire
    you? Hope, resistance

24. Do you associate specific concepts with
    the subject? Resilience, resistance,
    uniqueness, survival

25. Is there any text in the image? No

EXAMPLE 2

1. What is the primary subject of the image? Baby, pram

2. Are there synonyms to describe the subject? Carriage

3. How is the subject called in other languages? Carrozzina, kinderwagen, lastenvaunut

4. What are the secondary subjects of the image? Church, cathedral, grass, architecture

5. What is the name of the secondary subjects in other languages? Chiesa, Kirche, cattedrale, tuomiokirkko

6. What is the main color of the subjects? Red, green, grey

7. Do the subjects have a specific shape? Columns

8. In which situation was the image taken? Day, spring

9. Was the image taken in a specific history moment? No

10. Has the subject a specific use nowadays? Walking, transportation, childcare

11. Has the subject a traditional use? Childcare

12. What's the size of the image? Rectangle

13. What type of image is it? Color, digital

14. Which capturing device was used? Smartphone, Nokia

15. Is the image edited? No

16. Are there safety concerns associated? Collision, protection, terrorism

17. Female/ male subject? Gender-neutral

18. Where is the subject usually found? City, center

19. Can you imagine future applications for the subject? Money, safety, electric, animal, dog, transport

20. Has the image any relation to current events? Parenting, Abortion, overpopulation, conservationism, Catholicism, architecture

21. Has the image any relation to past events? No

22. Do you associate specific smells with the subject? Grass

23. Which feelings does the image inspire you? Hope, familiarity

24. Do you associate specific concepts with the subject? Family, genetics, excess, history, generations, time

25. Is there any text in the image? No

EXAMPLE 3

1. What is the primary subject of the image? Graffiti

2. Are there synonyms to describe the subject? Inscription

3. How is the subject called in other languages? Grafiti, seinäkirjoitukset

4. What is the secondary subject of the image? Surface

5. What is the name of the secondary subjects in other languages? Superficie, Oberfläche , Mauer

6. What is the main color of the subjects? Pink, green

7. Do the subjects have a specific shape? No

8. In which situation was the image taken?- A walk

9. Was the image taken in a specific history moment? Frauenstreik, 2019, Switzerland

10. Has the subject a specific use nowadays? Poster

11. Has the subject a traditional use? No

12. What's the size of the image? Rectangle

13. What type of image is it? Color, digital, focused

14. Which capturing device was used? Smartphone

15. Is the image edited? No

16. Are there safety concerns associated? Manifestation, security

17. Female/ male subject? Female

18. Where is the subject usually found? City

19. Can you imagine future applications for the subject? T-shirts, merchandising, portray

20. Has the image any relation to current events? Equality, rights, democracy

21. Has the image any relation to past events?
    Demonstration, equality, salary

22. Do you associate specific smells with the subject? No

23. Which feelings does the image inspire you? Rage, will, strength, resistance

24. Do you associate specific concepts with the subject? Purpose, activity, action, motivation, unite

25. Is there any text in the image? Streik, 14.6

DEDICATIONS

This pamphlet is dedicated to all the visitors of the Poetry from the lab blog, both to those who leave comments and those who leave immediately. I hope this work will be of help to you and to the whole community.

This short exploration of the world of tags and how a three-dimensional approach can be adopted Is dedicated to my husband that supported me working on it and my daughter that peacefully slept during the writing. This would have not been possible without both of your positive and heart-warming contribution. Your smiles always push me to step forward and challenge the status quo we live in together. We will grow together.

www.ingramcontent.com/pod-product-compliance
Lightning Source LLC
Chambersburg PA
CBHW041151050326
40689CB00004B/725